Vocabulary
Workbook

PEARSON

Scott
Foresman

Editorial Offices: Glenview, Illinois • Parsippany, New Jersey • New York, New York
Sales Offices: Parsippany, New Jersey • Duluth, Georgia • Glenview, Illinois
Coppell, Texas • Ontario, California • Mesa, Arizona

www.sfsocialstudies.com

ISBN 0-328-09069-7

Copyright © Pearson Education, Inc.

13 14 15 16 17   V011   16 15 14 13 12

© Scott Foresman 5

Looking at Words

Good Guides

Words in a dictionary are listed in alphabetical order. Guide words at the top of each page tell you the first and last words on the page. Using guide words can help you find the word you are looking for more quickly. Alphabetize your vocabulary cards. Then write each vocabulary word under its correct guide words.

1. adventure–civil

_____

_____

_____

2. client–construct

_____

_____

3. consult–curb

_____

_____

4. define–entry

_____

_____

_____

5. envelope–freeze

_____

_____

_____

_____

6. gauge–important

_____

_____

_____

_____

7. instead–noble

_____

_____

_____

8. noisy–prize

_____

_____

_____

9. produce–syllable

_____

_____

_____

_____

> **Notes for Home:** Today your child practiced alphabetizing the vocabulary words of this unit.
> **Home Activity:** Have your child make a list of last names that begin with different letters and look up the names in a phone directory by using the guide words.

Name _____

Hidden Message

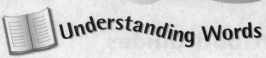

Understanding Words

Follow the steps on these two pages to help you figure out the hidden message at the end.

Step 1 On the lines below, write the vocabulary words next to the definitions. Use your vocabulary cards if you need help.

1. another word for growing food _____

2. a member of a country _____

3. protecting the environment _____

4. a written plan of government _____

5. a buyer or user of goods or services _____

6. way of life of a group of people _____

7. government run by the people _____

8. habitat _____

9. study of the earth and its use by people _____

10. important beliefs _____

11. people who have left one country to go to another _____

12. needing each other _____

13. a method of bringing water to dry land _____

14. silver nugget found in the earth, for example _____

15. something that dirties the air, water, or land _____

16. snow, rain, sleet, hail _____

17. a government of elected representatives _____

18. weather in an area over a long period of time _____

19. a count of the population _____

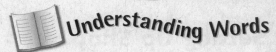
Step 2 Now find and circle the vocabulary words in the puzzle below. Use the answers from page 2 to help you find the words. The words are hidden forward, backward, up, and down. Some words share letters.

```
A T N E M N O R I V N E T H P
G E E N T R E P R E N E U R R
R N G E O G R A P H Y I S D E
I O C I L B U P E R T H E E C
C I T I Z E N L A R E N I M I
U T C O R N E R S T O N E O P
L U N O I T A V R E S N O C I
T T O F T H E F R E E N R T
U I M M I G R A N T S T E A A
R T I R R I G A T I O N R C T
E S L A E D I P R I S E E Y I
I N T E R D E P E N D E N T O
C O O N C O N S U M E R O M N
Y C U L T U R E E T A M I L C
N O I T U L L O P C E N S U S
```

Step 3 In order from left to right, write the letters that were not circled on the spaces below. A hidden message will be revealed.

_ _ _   _ _ _ _ _ _ _ _ _ _ _ _   _ _   _ _ _ _

_ _ _ _ _ _ _ _ _ _ _   _ _   _ _ _   _ _ _ _

_ _ _ _ _ _ _   _ _ _ _ _ _ _ .

Notes for Home: Today your child learned the definitions for vocabulary words and followed steps to arrive at a hidden message.
Home Activity: Ask your child to read the hidden message to you. Discuss the meaning of the vocabulary words **entrepreneur** and **free enterprise** and think of examples in your community.

Setting Up Shop
Narrative Writing

Location is an important thing to think about when starting a business. Concerns such as what resources are available and how easy it is to transport a product are important ones when choosing a location for a new business. Suppose you are starting a business. Think about what kind of business you would like to start and what the best location would be to start your business. Write to explain how your business relates to where it is located. Use at least five words from the word box. You may use an additional sheet of paper.

agriculture	climate	economy	geography	environment
region	consumer	supply	demand	entrepreneur
import	export	profit	natural resource	free enterprise
renewable resource				

_____

_____

_____

_____

_____

_____

_____

_____

_____

_____

_____

Notes for Home: Today your child explained how he or she would go about choosing a location for a new business.
Home Activity: Invite your child to look up businesses in local newspaper advertisements and in local business directories. Discuss why these businesses might be successful in your community.

culture

ideals

ethnic group

census

immigrants

democracy

republic

constitution

citizen

© Scott Foresman 5

important beliefs

way of life of a group of people

count of the population

group of people who share the same customs and language

government that is run by the people

people who leave one country to go live in another country

Written plan of government. The United States Constitution, adopted in 1789, is the plan for the national government.

form of government in which the people elect representatives to make laws and run the government

member of a country

private property	economy
free enterprise	profit
supply	demand
export	import
consumer	

system for producing and
distributing goods and services

something owned by
individual people

money a business has left over
after it has paid all its costs

economic system in which
people are free to start their
own businesses and own their
own property

amount of a product that people
are willing to buy

amount of a product that
is available

good that one country buys from
another country

good that one country sells to
another country

person who buys or uses goods
and services

entrepreneur	**region**
geography	**agriculture**
irrigation	**climate**
precipitation	**interdependent**

large area that has common features that set it apart from other areas

person who starts a new business, hoping to make a profit

business of growing crops and raising animals

study of Earth and how people use it

weather in an area over a long period of time

method of bringing water to dry land

needing each other

moisture that falls to Earth in the form of rain, snow, or sleet

natural resource

mineral

fossil fuel

renewable
resource

nonrenewable
resource

conservation

environment

pollution

substance such as gold, copper, or salt that is found in the earth and is not a plant or animal

something found in nature that people can use

resource that can be renewed or replaced, such as a tree

fuel, such as coal, oil, or natural gas, that is formed from the remains of plants and animals that lived thousands of years ago

protection and careful use of natural resources

resource that cannot be easily replaced, such as a fossil fuel

something that dirties the water, air, or soil

all things that surround us, such as land, water, air, and trees

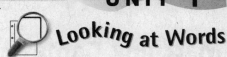

Are We Related?

Each of the words below is related to one of the vocabulary words in this unit.
Look at each word. Then use the vocabulary cards to help you find related words.
Saying the words aloud to see how alike they sound can be helpful. For each word
below, write the related vocabulary word.

1. migratory _____

2. pilgrim _____

3. archaeology _____

4. navigate _____

5. civilized _____

6. culture _____

7. reserve _____

8. ceremonial _____

9. special _____

10. attributed _____

11. theorize _____

12. dislodge _____

This unit has two pairs of word relatives. Use your cards to help find the word
relatives. Then write the words below.

13. _____ _____

14. _____ _____

List two pairs of word relatives that you know in the spaces below.

15. _____ _____

16. _____ _____

Notes for Home: Today your child identified words that are related to some of this unit's
vocabulary words.
Home Activity: Help your child to make a list of other words that are related to the words on
this page. For example, to *migratory,* you may add *migration, emigrate,* and *immigrate.*

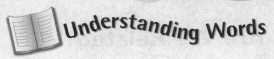

Matching Game

Understanding Words

Play this game with a partner. Each player needs a set of vocabulary cards on which is written his or her name.

Player 1: Stack all your vocabulary cards in a pile, word side up.

Player 2: Place all your vocabulary cards in a line, in any order, with the definition side up.

Player 1: Take the top card from the stack of cards with the word side up. Find the definition you feel matches the word. If the word and definition match, take the pair. If not, put the word card at the bottom of the stack and the definition card back in the line.

Player 2: Repeat the same steps as Player 1.

Keep playing by taking turns until there are no more cards to match. The player who has the most pairs at the end of the game is the winner.

Repeat the game until each player can match all the words and definitions. Then each player is a winner!

Ice Age	glacier	migrate	theory
artifact	archaeologist	ceremony	mesa
drought	civilization	surplus	specialize
pyramid	empire	tribute	slavery
tribe	league	cultural region	longhouse
wampum	reservation	lodge	tepee
travois	powwow	pueblo	potlatch
totem pole	shaman	emperor	magnetic compass
caravan	pilgrimage	astrolabe	saga
Renaissance	navigation	slave trade	

Notes for Home: Your child matched vocabulary words with definitions.
Home Activity: With your child, go over the words in this unit. Have him or her give you his or her own explanations of the words and then tell how they relate to the subjects of the unit.

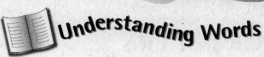
Understanding Words

Words From Other Languages

The English language has many words that come from other languages. In this unit, there are many vocabulary words that come from Native American languages. Others come from Spanish, Latin, Greek, Norse, and French. Write the vocabulary word on the line that matches its clue. Use the vocabulary cards to help you find the words.

Native American Words

1. a Native American word for polished shells and beads used for trading and

   sending messages _____

2. a Native American word for a home made of poles and buffalo hide

   _____

3. a Native American word for a ceremony with dancing and games

   _____

Norse Words

4. a Norse word that means "long story" _____

French and Canadian French Words

5. a Canadian French word that describes something used for hauling loads

   _____

6. a French word meaning "rebirth" (used to name a period of a rebirth of interest

   in learning in Europe) _____

Spanish Words

7. a Spanish word for "village" _____

8. a Spanish word for "high, flat landform" _____

© Scott Foresman 5

 Notes for Home: Your child identified vocabulary words that come from other languages.
Home Activity: With your child, think of other words from foreign languages that people use in everyday conversation.

Ways of Life
Expository Writing

The ways of life developed by Native Americans varied in the different regions of North America. Suppose that you could travel back in time to a Native American village. Choose a region you would like to visit. Think about the different ways of life that developed in that region. Write a journal entry to describe your visit and the unique ways of life of the people of that region. Use as many vocabulary words as you can. You may use an additional sheet of paper.

ceremony	tribe	wampum	reservation	longhouse
tepee	travois	powwow	pueblo	potlatch
totem pole	shaman	caravan	drought	magnetic compass

_____

_____

_____

_____

_____

_____

_____

_____

_____

_____

_____

_____

_____

_____

 Notes for Home: Today your child wrote a journal entry describing what a visit to a Native American village would be like.
Home Activity: Ask your child to describe the things in his or her life that are affected by or unique to the area where you live.

Ice Age

glacier

migrate

theory

artifact

archaeologist

ceremony

mesa

thick sheets of ice that covered the Earth's surface during the Ice Age

period during which low temperatures caused large areas of Earth's water to freeze

one possible explanation for something

to move from one area to another

scientist who studies the artifacts of people who lived long ago and draws conclusions from them

object made by people in the past

high, flat landform that rises steeply from the land around it

activity done for a special purpose

✂

drought	civilization
surplus	specialize
pyramid	empire
tribute	slavery

culture with organized systems of government, religion, and learning

long period without rain

focus on one particular product, activity, or job

more than is needed

large group of lands and peoples ruled by one leader

building with three or more sides shaped like triangles that slant toward a point at the top

practice of owning people and forcing them to work

payment a ruler demands from people he or she rules

tribe

league

cultural region

longhouse

wampum

reservation

lodge

tepee

union of people or groups

group of families bound together under a single leadership

building used for shelter by Iroquois

area in which people with similar cultures live

land set aside by the United States government for Native Americans

belts or strings of polished seashells that were used for trading and gift-giving by Iroquois and other Native Americans

dwelling built by Plains Indians, made of poles arranged in a circle covered by buffalo hides

large, round hut built by Plains Indians

travois	powwow
pueblo	potlatch
totem pole	shaman
emperor	magnetic compass

© Scott Foresman 5

Native American ceremony that often includes traditional dancing and games

sled made of poles tied together; used by Native Americans to transport goods across the plains

Native American celebration in which the hosts give gifts to their guests

Spanish word for "village"

Native American doctor or healer

wooden post carved with animals or other images; often made by Native Americans of the Pacific Northwest to honor ancestors or special events

Chinese invention that aided navigation by showing which direction was north

ruler of an empire

caravan

pilgrimage

astrolabe

saga

Renaissance

navigation

slave trade

journey taken for religious reasons	group of traders traveling
long, spoken tale repeated from one generation to the next	navigational tool that helped sailors use the sun and stars to find their way
science used by sailors to plot their course and determine their location	period in Europe beginning in about 1350 during which there was a new desire to learn more about the arts, sciences, and other parts of the world
	buying and selling of human beings

All in the Ending

Suffixes are word parts that are added to the end of a word to change the meaning of the word. Look at the following examples of suffixes:

-*ary* means "a person or thing connected with"
   For example: *second<u>ary</u>*

-*er, -or* means "one who"
   For example: *bak<u>er</u>, teach<u>er</u>, act<u>or</u>*

-*ist* means "one who does, makes, or practices"
   For example: *art<u>ist</u>, dent<u>ist</u>*

-*ion* means "act of" or "state of"
   For example: *act<u>ion</u>, concentrat<u>ion</u>*

Add one of these suffixes to each word below to create one of this unit's vocabulary words. Use the vocabulary cards to help you. Remember: When a word ends in *e* or *y*, you may need to drop the *e* or *y* before adding a suffix.

1. persecute _____

2. mission _____

3. debt _____

4. colony _____

5. dissent _____

6. separate _____

7. expedite _____

8. proprietary _____

List as many other words you know that end with the above suffixes.

_____

_____

Notes for Home: Your child learned to attach suffix endings to words to create some of this unit's vocabulary words.
Home Activity: With your child, think of other words that use any of the above suffixes. Have your child explain the meaning of the words to you.

Letter from New Spain

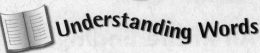
Understanding Words

Complete the letter to the king and queen of Spain from a Spanish governor in North America. Use the correct words from the word box.

cash crop	colony	convert	persecuted
encomienda	expedition	missionary	plantation

Your Royal Highnesses,

Our efforts to create a Spanish _____ for settlers in New Spain have been successful. Our local _____ is teaching Christianity to the natives. He has convinced many to _____ to our religion.

Señor Blanco sends thanks for your _____ that gave him control over the locals on his land. He is using the land for a large _____ where he will grow cocoa as a _____ to be sold in Spain.

We are planning an _____ to explore the wilderness. We will send some priests along to protect the natives we meet from being _____.

Your humble servant,
Eduardo Ortiz

Notes for Home: Today your child used context clues to help complete sentences with vocabulary words from this unit.
Home Activity: Challenge your child to use other vocabulary words to write his or her own letter to the king of England about life in a *British* colony in America. Have your child leave blanks where vocabulary words belong. Talk about the words that belong in the blanks.

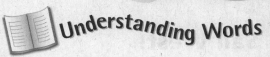

Twenty Questions

Understanding Words

Work with a partner. Use one set of vocabulary cards. Place all of the cards in a container. Player 1 draws a card and holds it so Player 2 cannot see it. Player 2 can ask twenty "yes" or "no" questions to try to figure out what vocabulary word Player 1 is holding. Players switch roles each time.

As you play, be sure to tally the number of questions you ask. When you have guessed the word, or asked all twenty questions, write down the word in the blank and the number of questions it took to guess it. If you were unable to guess the word, your score for that word is 25.

When each player has guessed five words, add up the total number of questions you asked. The player who asked the **least** number of questions is the winner.

Player 1

Word	Questions
1.	
2.	
3.	
4.	
5.	
Total	

Player 2

Word	Questions
1.	
2.	
3.	
4.	
5.	
Total	

Notes for Home: Today your child reviewed the meanings of the vocabulary words by playing a guessing game with a partner.
Home Activity: Work with your child to use this unit's vocabulary words to create a short skit about a character and setting from colonial times. Act out the skit with your child.

Sail West!
Persuasive Writing

The English colonies were established in North America for a number of reasons. Some were started for religious reasons. Others were started for economic reasons. Suppose you could start your own colony. Think of the advantages of living in the colony instead of living in England. Write an advertisement to persuade people in England to move to your colony. Use at least three words from the vocabulary box. You may use an additional sheet of paper.

dissenter	ally	cash crop	charter	colonist
House of Burgesses	expedition	plantation	pilgrim	Puritan
Mayflower Compact	persecution	proprietor	Separatist	stock
Northwest Passage				

_____

_____

_____

_____

_____

_____

_____

_____

_____

_____

_____

Notes for Home: Today your child wrote a persuasive advertisement to encourage people to leave England to live in a colony in North America.
Home Activity: Discuss with your child the different reasons people today may move from one state to another state or from one country to another country.

Vocabulary Workbook

expedition	**colony**
Columbian Exchange	**conquistador**
ally	**conquest**
convert	

settlement far from the country that rules it

journey made for a special purpose

Spanish word for conquerors who came to the Americas in the 1500s

movement of people, animals, plants, diseases, and ways of life between the Eastern Hemisphere and Western Hemisphere following the voyages of Columbus

capture or taking of something by force

a friend who will help in a fight

to change from one belief to another

colonist

society

plantation

encomienda

missionary

mission

charter

group of people forming
a community

person who lives in a colony

Grant given by the King of Spain
to wealthy settlers in New Spain.
Gave settlers control of all the
Native Americans living on
an area of land.

large farm with many workers who
live on the land they work

religious settlement where
missionaries live and work

person who teaches his or her
religion to others who have
different beliefs

official document giving a person
or group permission to do
something

© Scott Foresman 5

stock	cash crop
indentured servant	House of Burgesses
Northwest Passage	pilgrim
Separatists	

© Scott Foresman 5

crop grown to be sold for profit	share in a company
law-making assembly in colonial Virginia	person who agreed to work for someone for a certain amount of time in exchange for the cost of the voyage to North America
person who travels to a new place for religious reasons	water route that explorers hoped would flow through North America, connecting the Atlantic and Pacific oceans
	Group of people from England who wanted to separate themselves from the Church of England. Some traveled to North America in search of religious freedom.

persecution

Mayflower Compact

Puritan

dissenter

proprietor

debtor

plan of government written
by the Pilgrims who sailed on
the *Mayflower*

unjust treatment because of
one's beliefs

person whose views differ from
those of his or her leaders

Group of people who wanted to
"purify" the Church of England.
They established the Massachusetts
Bay Colony in 1630.

person who owes money

owner

Break It Up

It can be easier to read and spell new words, short or long, when you break them up into syllables. Remember, a syllable is a part of a word in which we hear a vowel sound. Here are some examples of how words can be broken into syllables:

- Break between double consonants. Example: *sum - mer*.
- Sometimes break between two different consonants. Example: *par - ty*.
- Sometimes a vowel stands alone. Example: *choc - o - late*.

Put the words from the word box in alphabetical order and write them on the lines below. Then, next to each word, write the word in syllables. Use a dictionary to check your answers.

apprentice	artisan	tributary	almanac
Middle Passage	self-sufficient	town common	trading post
Great Awakening	backcountry	triangular trade routes	

Alphabetical Order   **Word in Syllables**

1. _____   _____

2. _____   _____

3. _____   _____

4. _____   _____

5. _____   _____

6. _____   _____

7. _____   _____

8. _____   _____

9. _____   _____

10. _____   _____

11. _____   _____

Notes for Home: Today your child put the vocabulary words from this unit in alphabetical order and broke each word into syllables.
Home Activity: Have your child put your music, book, recipe, or other collection in alphabetical order.

Name _____

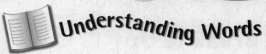

UNIT 3

Working with Synonyms

Understanding Words

A synonym is a word that means the same, or nearly the same, as another word. Read the list of vocabulary words and the list of synonyms. Write the letter of the synonym beside the word it matches.

Vocabulary Words

Synonyms

1. apprentice _____

a. large estate

2. artisan _____

b. river branch

3. self-sufficient _____

c. wilderness

4. town common _____

d. fort

5. almanac _____

e. self-reliant

6. hacienda _____

f. town square

7. presidio _____

g. student

8. trading post _____

h. craftsperson

9. tributary _____

i. reference book

10. backcountry _____

j. backcountry market

 Notes for Home: Today your child found synonyms for some of this unit's vocabulary words.
Home Activity: Choose a synonym from the list on this page. Invite your child to say the vocabulary word that matches it. Continue until your child has named vocabulary words for all the synonyms.

© Scott Foresman 5

Name That Event

Read the sentences below. Each one describes an event named in this unit. Write the correct name of the event described. Use the vocabulary cards if you need help.

Proclamation of 1763	**El Camino Real**	**Stono Rebellion**
Pontiac's Rebellion	**King Philip's War**	**Great Awakening**
Pueblo Revolt	**French and Indian War**	**Middle Passage**

1. Colonists felt religious excitement in the 1730s. _____

2. In the 1670s in New England, a war was fought between English settlers and Native Americans. _____

3. In 1763, French and Native Americans teamed up against the British forces but lost. _____

4. This was the second leg of the way, from West Africa to the West Indies. _____

5. In the late 1600s, the villagers organized and drove out their Spanish conquerors in what is now New Mexico. _____

6. Mistreated plantation workers took matters into their own hands in 1739, but paid with their lives. _____

7. You did not have to be a king or queen to travel on this colonial royal road that linked the Spanish colonies to Mexico. _____

8. This chief's attacks against British forts and settlements in 1763 made an English king sit up and take notice. _____

9. Already unpopular in North America, King George III's statement prohibiting new settlement west of the Appalachian Mountains made him no new friends among the settlers. _____

Notes for Home: Today your child identified historical events with vocabulary words from this unit.
Home Activity: Choose one of the vocabulary words from the word box. Invite your child to tell you more about that event.

Life in the Colonies
Narrative Writing

Many American colonists left everything they had back in England to start a new life. Moving brought new opportunities, but also meant leaving friends and family behind. Suppose you just moved to the colonies from England. Think about what you have learned about colonial life. Write a letter back to your cousin in England to describe what your life is like in the colonies. Use as many vocabulary words as you can. You may use an additional sheet of paper.

apprentice	**town common**	**self-sufficient**
trading post	**backcountry**	**tributary**
French and Indian War	**artisan**	**almanac**
Proclamation of 1763		

_____

_____

_____

_____

_____

_____

_____

_____

_____

_____

_____

_____

 Notes for Home: Today your child wrote a letter from the point of view of a child who moved to the American colonies from England.
Home Activity: Discuss with your child the differences between life today and life in colonial times. Ask how daily life would be different for your family if you lived in colonial times.

apprentice

artisan

triangular trade routes

Middle Passage

self-sufficient

town common

Great Awakening

skilled worker who makes things

young person who learns a skill from a more experienced worker

name given to the second leg of the triangular trade routes; extended from West Africa to the West Indies

three-sided trade route between the 13 Colonies, the West Indies, and Africa; included the slave trade

open space in the center of many New England and Middle Colony towns where cattle and sheep could graze

ability to rely on oneself for most of what one needs

Important religious movement among Christians that began in the colonies in the 1730s. This movement revived many colonists' interest in religion.

✂

almanac

Stono Rebellion

hacienda

presidio

El Camino Real

Pueblo Revolt

trading post

slave rebellion in South Carolina in 1739

reference book with helpful facts and figures

military fort built by the Spanish

large estates built by wealthy Spanish ranchers in North America

Native American revolt in the late 1600s in which the Pueblo temporarily drove the Spanish out of New Mexico

Spanish for "the royal road," a route that linked Spain's colonies in the American Southwest with Mexico

place in colonial North America where settlers and Native Americans met to trade

tributary

King Philip's War

backcountry

French and Indian War

Pontiac's Rebellion

Proclamation of 1763

war in 1670s between Native
Americans and English settlers
living in New England

stream or river that flows into
a large river

war fought by the British
against the French and their
Native American allies in North
America, which was won by the
British in 1763

in the 13 Colonies the
rugged stretch of land near
the Appalachian Mountains

law issued by King George III
stating that colonists were no
longer allowed to settle on land
west of the Appalachian Mountains

Native American rebellion led by
the Ottawa leader Pontiac in 1763

Name _____

Common and Proper Nouns

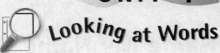

Looking at Words

Nouns name people, places, and things. A common noun names any person, place, or thing. A proper noun names a particular or certain person, place, or thing. A proper noun always begins with a capital letter.

Read the sentences below. Underline the vocabulary words that are common nouns. Circle the vocabulary words that are proper nouns.

1. Because of the **Stamp Act**, a colonist had to pay a tax when he bought a newspaper.

2. A **tariff** was paid as a tax on tea from Britain.

3. British soldiers killed five people during the **Boston Massacre**.

4. Under the **Tea Act** the colonists had to buy all their tea from one company.

5. The colonists dumped British tea into the harbor during the **Boston Tea Party**.

6. The **American Revolution** was fought to gain independence from Britain.

7. The **minutemen** were ready to fight for the colonies as soon as they were called.

8. The colonies explained why they wanted to be free in the **Declaration of Independence**.

The proper noun **American Revolution** is a particular example of the common noun *war*. In the sentences below, the underlined word is a common noun. For each, complete the sentence by writing a particular proper noun example. There may be more than one answer. The first sentence has been completed for you.

9. _____Virginia_____ was one of the thirteen original <u>colonies</u>.

10. The _____ was a British <u>law</u> that angered the colonists.

11. _____ was an important colonial <u>leader</u>.

Notes for Home: Today your child learned to identify common and proper nouns.
Home Activity: Have your child make a list of common nouns by writing the names of household appliances and products. Then have your child write the name of the manufacturer of each product to generate a list of proper nouns.

Name My Name

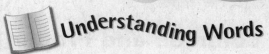
Understanding Words

Write the word from the word box that names the person or group defined by each statement. Use the vocabulary cards to help you.

Sons of Liberty	militia	traitor	Parliament
Patriots	mercenary	minutemen	Loyalists
Continental Army	Daughters of Liberty		

1. I fought battles for money. _____

2. We burned stamps and attacked stamp agents. _____

3. We were soldiers from all 13 colonies. _____

4. We passed laws to tax the colonies. _____

5. We women wove our own cloth. _____

6. I betrayed my country. _____

7. We were the colonists who were against British rule. _____

8. We were the colonists who supported King George. _____

9. We volunteered to fight the British. _____

10. We were ready to fight the minute we were called. _____

Notes for Home: Today your child identified people and groups relating to the American Revolution.
Home Activity: Discuss with your child what patriotism meant to both sides of the American Revolution. Start the discussion by suggesting that each side felt that it was patriotic.

When and What Happened?

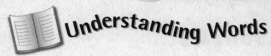

Understanding Words

Find the vocabulary cards for the words in the word box. Then put the cards in chronological order, starting from the earliest event to the latest event. On the lines below, write the vocabulary words in the order in which they occurred. Include a brief description of what happened.

Battle of Bunker Hill	**First Continental Congress**	**Battle of Saratoga**
Olive Branch Petition	**Second Continental Congress**	**Treaty of Paris**

1. _____

   _____

2. _____

   _____

3. _____

   _____

4. _____

   _____

5. _____

   _____

6. _____

   _____

Notes for Home: Your child put in chronological order events from this unit's vocabulary words.

Home Activity: Ask your child to tell you which of the events on this page he or she thinks were the most important. Ask your child to explain why.

Join Us!

Persuasive Writing

The events of the 1770s caused British colonists to suddenly find themselves having to make a choice—remain loyal to Britain, or join the colonists who wanted to break away from Britain. Suppose you are a colonist living in Boston, Massachusetts, in 1775. Think about the reasons for and the reasons against breaking away from Britain. Write a persuasive speech to read to your fellow colonists that explains your opinion and why you feel that way. Use at least five words from the word box. You may use an additional sheet of paper.

Parliament	Stamp Act	repeal	Sons of Liberty
Townshend Acts	tariff	boycott	Daughters of Liberty
Boston Massacre	Tea Act	Patriots	Loyalists
Boston Tea Party	Intolerable Acts	Committee of Correspondence

_____

_____

_____

_____

_____

_____

_____

_____

_____

_____

_____

_____

_____

Notes for Home: Today your child wrote a persuasive speech saying whether or not the American colonists should revolt against Great Britain.
Home Activity: Ask your child how he or she went about making a choice. Work with your child to come up with another situation in which making a list of pros and cons could help make a decision.

Parliament

Stamp Act

repeal

Sons of Liberty

Townshend Acts

tariff

boycott

Daughters of Liberty

law passed by Parliament in 1765 that taxed printed materials in the 13 Colonies	Britain's law-making assembly
groups of Patriots who worked to oppose British rule before the American Revolution	to cancel
tax on imported goods	laws passed by Parliament in 1767 that taxed goods imported by the 13 Colonies from Britain
groups of American women Patriots who wove cloth to replace boycotted British goods	organized refusal to buy goods

Vocabulary Workbook

Boston Massacre

Committee of Correspondence

Tea Act

Boston Tea Party

Intolerable Acts

Patriots

Loyalists

groups of colonists formed in the 1770s to spread news quickly about protests against the British

event in 1770 in Boston in which British soldiers killed five colonists who were part of an angry group that had surrounded them

protest against British taxes in which the Sons of Liberty boarded British ships and dumped tea into Boston Harbor in 1773

law passed by Parliament in the early 1770s stating that only the East India Company, a British business, could sell tea to the 13 Colonies

American colonists who opposed British rule

laws passed by British Parliament to punish the people of Boston following the Boston Tea Party

colonists who remained loyal to the British during the American Revolution

First Continental Congress

militia

minutemen

American Revolution

Battle of Bunker Hill

Second Continental Congress

Continental Army

✂

	meeting of representatives from every colony except Georgia, held in Philadelphia in 1774 to discuss actions to take in response to the Intolerable Acts
volunteer armies	
the war between the 13 Colonies and Great Britain from 1775 to 1783 in which the 13 Colonies won their independence and became the United States	colonial militia groups that could be ready to fight at a minute's notice
congress of American leaders which first met in 1775, declared independence in 1776, and helped lead the United States during the Revolution	costly victory for British troops over the Patriots in Charlestown, Massachusetts, in the American Revolution on June 17, 1775
	army formed in 1775 by the Second Continental Congress and led by General George Washington

Olive Branch Petition

Declaration of Independence

traitor

Green Mountain Boys

mercenary

Battle of Saratoga

Treaty of Paris

document declaring the 13 American colonies independent of Great Britain, written mainly by Thomas Jefferson and adopted on July 4, 1776, by the Second Continental Congress

letter sent by the Second Continental Congress to King George III in 1775 in an attempt to avoid war

group of Vermont soldiers who captured Fort Ticonderoga in 1775

person who works against his or her country

American victory over British troops in 1777 that was a turning point in the American Revolution

soldiers from one country who are paid to fight for another country

Treaty signed in 1783 that officially ended the American Revolution. Great Britain recognized the United States as an independent country.

Vocabulary Workbook

More Suffixes

When a suffix is added to a word, the meaning of the word changes. If the word ends with an *e*, drop the *e* before you add a suffix that begins with a vowel.

graduate + *-ion* = graduation   science + *-ist* = scientist

advance + *-ment* = advancement   relate + *-ive* = relative

fiction + *-al* = fictional

The vocabulary words in the word box each end with a suffix. Each definition below contains the root word for the vocabulary word it defines. Circle each root word. Then write the correct vocabulary word on the line that follows its definition. Check your vocabulary cards to see if your answers are correct.

national anthem	electoral college	executive branch
legislative branch	inauguration	amendment
Federalists	inflation	

This part of government must (execute) the law. ___executive branch___

1. We usually hold this ceremony to inaugurate the President in January.

_____

2. This is the official song that represents our nation. _____

3. This must be added to the Constitution to amend it. _____

4. These people believed in a federal system with a strong national government.

_____

5. The power of this part of government is to legislate. _____

6. This is the situation when prices inflate. _____

7. Each elector is chosen by his or her state to vote for President as part of this

group. _____

Notes for Home: Today your child learned how some of the unit's vocabulary words are built from suffixes and root words.
Home Activity: Look through books and magazines and ask your child to point out words with the suffix *-ion*, *-ist*, *-ment*, *-ive*, or *-al*. Have your child identify the root word for each word he or she finds.

Crossword

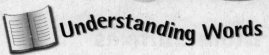

Use your vocabulary cards and clues from the unit to complete the crossword on page 63.

Across

1. The First Amendment through the Tenth Amendment

3. Slave population-count agreement

6. They wanted a weaker national government

7. An order to divide land: _____ of 1787

9. Where no one has settled

10. A plan to give all states an equal number of representatives

11. Words in support of the Constitution

12. A plan to give big states more representatives

16. Where the Shawnee fought bravely

17. French land sale

18. Agreement to make two houses

Down

1. Jackson beats the British

2. Farmers fight high taxes

4. One of the first to settle

5. Group of like-minded people: _____ party

7. Not for or against

8. Were ready to fight the British

13. Constitution's first words

14. The President's department heads

15. United States vs. Britain: _____ of 1812

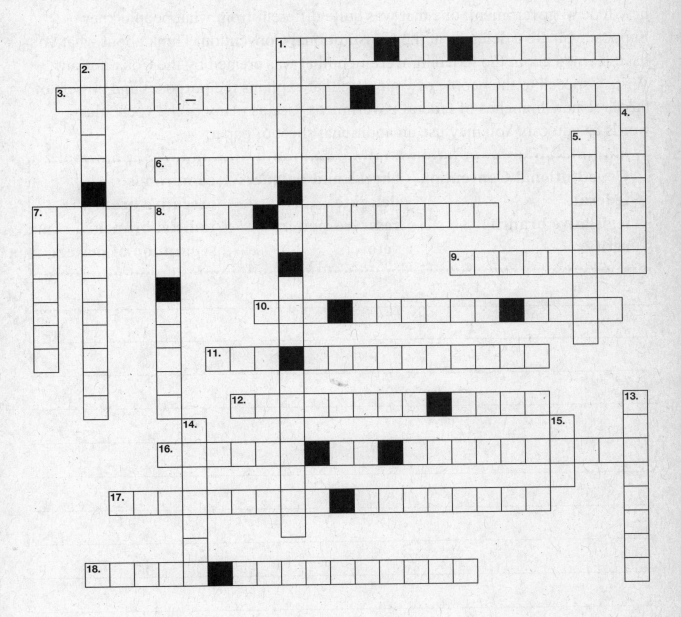

Notes for Home: Today your child completed a crossword puzzle using this unit's vocabulary words.
Home Activity: Ask your child to draw a picture of an event or to draw a diagram of an idea based on the vocabulary used in the crossword. Encourage your child to explain the event or idea to you.

A Conventional Letter
Expository Writing

One of the greatest accomplishments of the U.S. Constitution was its creation of a new federal government, one that was quite different from what people knew. Suppose you are a delegate at the Constitutional Convention. Think about what you have learned about the federal government that was created by the Constitution. Write a speech to the people of your state that explains the purposes and powers of the three new branches of federal government. Use as many of the vocabulary words as you can. You may use an additional sheet of paper.

Constitutional Convention	**checks and balances**	**compromise**
federal	**delegate**	**executive branch**
legislative branch	**reserved powers**	**judicial branch**
ratify	**veto**	**separation of powers**

_____

_____

_____

_____

_____

_____

_____

_____

_____

_____

_____

 Notes for Home: Today your child wrote a letter explaining the three branches of the federal government.
Home Activity: Discuss with your child how the rights and freedoms guaranteed by the Bill of Rights are practiced today. Find newspaper or magazine articles that describe how these rights and freedoms are protected by the three branches of government.

Articles of Confederation	ratify
legislative branch	executive branch
judicial branch	inflation
Shays' Rebellion	Northwest Ordinance of 1787

to officially approve

First plan of government for the United States, in effect from 1781 to 1789. It gave more power to the states than to the central government.

part of the government, headed by the President, that carries out the laws

part of the government that passes laws

economic condition in which prices rise very quickly

part of the government that decides the meaning of laws

federal order that divided the Northwest Territory into smaller territories and created a plan for how the territories could become states

revolt of Massachusetts's farmers against high state taxes, led by Daniel Shays

✂

delegate	Constitutional Convention
Virginia Plan	New Jersey Plan
compromise	Great Compromise
Three-Fifths Compromise	Preamble

meeting of delegates who met in Philadelphia, Pennsylvania, in 1787 and replaced the Articles of Confederation with the Constitution

person chosen to represent others

proposal during the Constitutional Convention that each state should have the same number of representatives in Congress

proposal during the Constitutional Convention that Congress be given greater power over the states and that large states have more representatives in Congress than small

agreement at the Constitutional Convention to create a Congress with two houses, first proposed by Roger Sherman of Connecticut

settlement of a disagreement in which each side agrees to give up part of its demands

introduction to the Constitution, beginning, "We the People of the United States…"

agreement made at the Constitutional Convention that only three-fifths of the slaves in a state would be counted for representation and tax purposes

✂

reserved powers	separation of powers
checks and balances	veto
Federalists	federal
Antifederalists	The Federalist

division of power among the three branches of the federal government under the Constitution

powers in the Constitution that are left to the individual states

power of the President to reject a bill passed by Congress

system set up by the Constitution that gives each branch of government the power to check, or limit, the power of the other branches

refers to the national government

supporters of a strong national government and in favor of adopting the Constitution

series of essays in 1787 and 1788 by James Madison, Alexander Hamilton, and John Jay that urged support of the new Constitution

people opposed to the new U.S. Constitution and its emphasis on a strong national government

✂

amendment	Bill of Rights
electoral college	inauguration
Cabinet	political party
pioneer	frontier

first ten amendments to the
Constitution, ratified in 1791

a change, or addition, to
the Constitution

ceremony in which a newly-elected
President takes office

group of people chosen by the
people of each state who vote
for President

organized group of people
who share similar views of
what government should do

officials appointed by the
President as advisers and to
head the departments in the
executive branch

outer edge of a settled area

early settler of a region

Louisiana Purchase

neutral

Battle of Tippecanoe

War Hawks

War of 1812

national anthem

Battle of New Orleans

not taking sides

territory purchased by the United States from France in 1803, extending from the Mississippi River to the Rocky Mountains and from the Gulf of Mexico to Canada

members of Congress who supported war with Britain in 1812

battle between United States soldiers and the Shawnee in 1811 that neither side won

Official song of a country. "The Star-Spangled Banner" is the national anthem of the United States.

conflict between the United States and Britain that lasted from 1812 to 1815

victory of United States forces commanded by Andrew Jackson over the British in the War of 1812

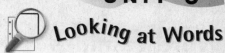
Predicting Meaning

Sometimes when you read a new vocabulary term, you may see familiar words that help you predict, or guess, what the term probably means. For example, you may predict that **Mexican War** means a fight with Mexico because you know the meanings of the words *war* and *Mexican*.

Predict the meaning of each vocabulary term below. Write your predictions in the "Prediction" column. Then use the vocabulary cards or glossary to see if you are correct. Check off the "Yes" or "No" column to keep track.

Vocabulary	Prediction	Yes	No
Indian Removal Act			
gold rush			
mountain men			
Trail of Tears			
Era of Good Feelings			
wagon train			

Notes for Home: Your child used familiar words to predict the meaning of some of this unit's vocabulary.
Home Activity: Help your child scan a magazine or newspaper article to find unfamiliar terms. Ask your child to predict meaning based on his or her knowledge of the words that make up each term.

Word Families

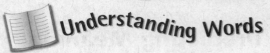Understanding Words

A word family is made up of words that are related to one another because they share word roots.

For the words in the word family below, read about the meaning of the root. For each of the words listed in the family, underline where you see the root. Then, explain how the root word helps you understand the definition. You may use a dictionary.

The vocabulary word **manufacture** is based on two Latin words. The word *manu* means "hand" and the word *facere* means "to do" or "to make."

Words with the root *manu*

1. **manufacture**

   Manufacture means "to make something by hand or machinery from raw

   materials." When you manufacture something, you may do it by hand.

2. manual

   _____

   _____

Words with the root *facere*

3. **manufacture**

   _____

   _____

4. artifact

   _____

   _____

 Notes for Home: Today your child built a word family for a vocabulary word from this unit.
Home Activity: Build word families from two familiar household items—*television* (roots: *tele* and *videre)* and *photograph* (roots: *photo* and *graph).*

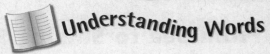

Headline News

Read the headlines for newspaper stories that could have been written about events from this unit. Write the words from the word box that relate to each headline.

cotton gin	Monroe Doctrine	Trail of Tears
suffrage	reform	temperance
canal	mechanical reaper	abolitionist
technology	Industrial Revolution	manufacture
nationalism	revival	Indian Removal Act
Era of Good Feelings	Seneca Falls Convention	

Native Americans Forced West

_____

_____

Monroe to World: Hands Off!

_____

_____

_____

Technologies Change the World

_____

_____

_____

_____

New Voices for Change

_____

_____

_____

_____

Notes for Home: Today your child sorted vocabulary words to reinforce their meanings.
Home Activity: Have your child read newspaper headlines to predict names, places, and terms that may be included in the articles. Read the articles together.

From Sea to Shining Sea?
Persuasive Writing

The rapid growth of the United States in the first half of the 1800s led to the idea of **manifest destiny.** As we grew, people wanted even more land. Westward movement meant more land and more resources, but it also meant taking land from Mexico and Native Americans. Think about the positive and negative aspects of U.S. westward movement. Write a persuasive paragraph supporting or opposing the U.S. policy of **manifest destiny.** Use as many of the vocabulary words as you can. You may use an additional sheet of paper.

nationalism	Indian Removal Act	Trail of Tears
Texas Revolution	annex	Mexican War
Bear Flag Revolt	Treaty of Guadalupe Hidalgo	wagon train
gold rush	forty-niners	discrimination

_____

_____

_____

_____

_____

_____

_____

_____

_____

_____

_____

Notes for Home: Your child wrote a persuasive paragraph supporting or opposing the policy of **manifest destiny.**
Home Activity: To see persuasive writing in action, have your child read the editorial section of the newspaper. Discuss the issues of the day and whether the writer's arguments are persuasive.

nationalism

Era of Good Feelings

Monroe Doctrine

suffrage

Indian Removal Act

Trail of Tears

Industrial Revolution

name given to the period after the War of 1812 marked by optimism, a geographically expanding country, and a growing economy

strong feeling of pride in one's country

right to vote

policy declared by President James Monroe warning European nations not to interfere in the Western Hemisphere

forced march of 15,000 Cherokee from the southeastern United States to Indian Territory in present-day Oklahoma in 1838

law passed in 1830 forcing American Indians living in the Southeast to be moved west of the Mississippi

period of important change in making goods by hand to making goods by machine in factories

✂

manufacture	technology
cotton gin	mechanical reaper
canal	reform
revival	

use of scientific knowledge or new tools to make or do something

to make goods from raw materials

machine invented by Cyrus McCormick that could harvest wheat quickly

machine invented by Eli Whitney that cleaned the seeds from cotton

change

human-made waterway

act of awakening or strengthening people's religious feelings

temperance

abolitionist

Seneca Falls
Convention

Texas Revolution

annex

manifest destiny

Mexican War

person who wants to abolish,
or end slavery

moderation, usually in drinking
of alcohol

war between Texas settlers and
Mexico from 1835 to 1836
resulting in the formation of
the Republic of Texas

first national convention on
women's rights, organized in 1848
by Lucretia Mott and Elizabeth
Cady Stanton

belief that the United States should
expand west to the Pacific Ocean

to add or attach

war lasting from 1846 to 1848
in which the United States
defeated Mexico and gained
Mexican territory

Bear Flag Revolt

Treaty of
Guadalupe Hidalgo

mountain men

wagon train

gold rush

forty-niner

discrimination

Treaty ending the Mexican War in 1848. Mexico gave up most of its northern territory to the United States in return for $15 million.

rebellion of California settlers against Mexican rule in 1846

common method of transportation to the West, in which wagons traveled in groups for safety

fur trappers who helped explore and settle the Oregon Country

nickname for a person who arrived in California in 1849 to look for gold

sudden movement of many people to an area where gold has been found

unfair treatment of a group or individual

Name _____

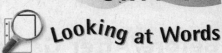

Look Inside

Use context clues and what you know about the underlined word or words in each vocabulary word to guess the meaning of that vocabulary word. Write your definition on the line below the sentence. When you are done, check your vocabulary cards to see if your definitions are correct.

1. The South was rebuilt during **Reconstruction**.

   Reconstruction: _____

2. Delaware was a **border state** between the North and the South.

   border state: _____

3. The **blockade** kept food from reaching the city.

   blockade: _____

4. Ohio was a **free state** in the North.

   free state: _____

5. **Sectionalism** divided people in different parts of the country.

   sectionalism: _____

6. Part of the food grown by **sharecropping** went to the landowner.

   sharecropping: _____

7. Georgia was a **slave state** in the South.

   slave state: _____

8. In **total war**, even people's homes are destroyed.

   total war: _____

9. The **Freedmen's Bureau** helped African Americans after the Civil War ended.

   Freedmen's Bureau: _____

10. Southerners felt that **states' rights** allowed them to have slavery where they lived.

    states' rights: _____

 Notes for Home: Today your child recognized words within this unit's vocabulary words and used them to predict meaning.
Home Activity: With your child, read a newspaper, magazine, or book. Look together for examples of words with base words that help to predict meaning.

Name _____

Before/After Game

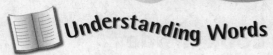Understanding Words

Play this game with a partner. Take out the vocabulary cards for the vocabulary words in the word box. Shuffle and stack the cards. Draw the two cards on top. Next to "Draw 1" below, write the events in the order you think they happened. The other player does the same. Continue to draw and order pairs of events until there are no more cards. Then you should both check your textbook to see if your answers are correct. Circle the event that happened first in each pair. The player with the most correct answers wins.

> **Battle of Antietam**   **Fugitive Slave Law**   **Fourteenth Amendment**
> **Battle of Gettysburg**   **Fifteenth Amendment**   **Missouri Compromise**
> **Kansas-Nebraska Act**   **Thirteenth Amendment**   **First Battle of Bull Run**
> **Emancipation Proclamation**

Draw 1: _____

_____

Draw 2: _____

_____

Draw 3: _____

_____

Draw 4: _____

_____

Draw 5: _____

_____

 Notes for Home: Today your child played a game in which he or she used vocabulary cards to put events surrounding the Civil War in chronological order.
Home Activity: Invite your child to put his or her day's events in chronological order and list them on paper.

Riddle Me This

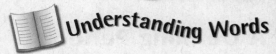

Understanding Words

Read the riddles below. Choose the answer to each riddle from the word box. Use the numbered letters to answer the riddle below.

Gettysburg Address	Fifteenth Amendment	Missouri Compromise
Freedmen's Bureau	Emancipation Proclamation	border states

1. I balanced slave states and free states. _____ _____ _____ _____ _____ _____ _____ _____
1 2 3 4 5 6 7 8

_____ _____ _____ _____ _____ _____ _____ _____ _____ _____
9 10 11 12 13 14 15 16 17 18

2. We were slave states that did not join the Confederacy.

_____ _____ _____ _____ _____ _____ _____ _____ _____ _____ _____ _____
19 20 21 22 23 24   25 26 27 28 29 30

3. My words during the Civil War freed all slaves.

_____ _____ _____ _____ _____ _____ _____ _____ _____ _____ _____ _____
31 32 33 34 35 36 37 38 39 40 41 42

_____ _____ _____ _____ _____ _____ _____ _____ _____ _____ _____ _____
43 44 45 46 47 48 49 50 51 52 53 54

4. I am Lincoln's famous speech. _____ _____ _____ _____ _____ _____ _____ _____ _____ _____
55 56 57 58 59 60 61 62 63 64

_____ _____ _____ _____ _____ _____ _____
65 66 67 68 69 70 71

5. I was established to help freed slaves after the war.

_____ _____ _____ _____ _____ _____ _____ _____ , _____ _____ _____ _____ _____ _____ _____
72 73 74 75 76 77 78 79   80   81 82 83 84 85 86

6. I gave all male citizens voting rights. _____ _____ _____ _____ _____ _____ _____ _____ _____
87 88 89 90 91 92 93 94 95

_____ _____ _____ _____ _____ _____ _____ _____ _____
96 97 98 99 100 101 102 103 104

What do Harriet Tubman's work and a subway system have in common? Each is...

_____ " _____ _____ _____ _____ _____ _____ _____ _____ _____ _____ _____ _____
27 79   6   93 66 18 83 55 24 5   62 103 22

_____ _____ _____ _____ _____ _____ _____ . "
44 96 40 47 68 10 33 76

Notes for Home: Today your child used vocabulary words to solve riddles about the Civil War.
Home Activity: With your child, take turns making up riddles that define other vocabulary words relating to the Civil War.

A Defining Period
Persuasive Writing

The period before, during, and after the Civil War is one of the most defining periods of U.S. history. Each event played an important role in shaping the future of our nation. Choose the event that you feel is the most important event of this time period. Write a persuasive essay about your choice. Use as many of the vocabulary words as you can. You may use an additional sheet of paper.

Emancipation Proclamation	**Fugitive Slave Law**	**slave state**
Underground Railroad	**Battle of Antietam**	**slave codes**
Fourteenth Amendment	**Gettysburg Address**	**free state**
First Battle of Bull Run	**Anaconda Plan**	**Union**
Battle of Gettyburg	**Jim Crow Laws**	**states' rights**
Battle of Vicksburg	**black codes**	**Confederacy**

_____

_____

_____

_____

_____

_____

_____

_____

_____

_____

Notes for Home: Today your child wrote about his or her choice for the most important event of the Civil War period.
Home Activity: Choose an article from a newspaper or magazine about a current event or listen to a story about such an event on the TV news. Discuss the event with your child and how it affects others.

sectionalism

slave codes

Underground Railroad

free state

slave state

states' rights

Missouri Compromise

Fugitive Slave Law

laws designed to control the behavior of enslaved people

loyalty to a part of a country rather than to a whole country

state in which slavery was not allowed

organized system of secret routes used by people escaping slavery, which led from the South to the North or Canada

idea that states have the right to make decisions about issues that concern them

state in which slavery was allowed

law passed in 1850 that said escaped slaves had to be returned to their owners even if they reached free states

law passed in 1820 that divided the Louisiana Territory into a southern area that allowed slavery and a northern area that did not

Compromise of 1850

Kansas-Nebraska Act

secede

Confederacy

Union

border state

civil war

law passed in 1854 allowing the people of these two territories to decide for themselves whether to allow slavery

law under which California was admitted to the Union as a free state and the Fugitive Slave Law was passed

Confederate States of America formed by the 11 Southern states that seceded from the Union after Abraham Lincoln was elected President

to break away from a group, as the Southern states broke away from the United States in 1861

during the Civil War, a state located between the Union and the Confederacy that allowed slavery but remained in the Union

states that remained loyal to the United States government during the Civil War

war between people of the same country

✂

blockade	**Anaconda Plan**
First Battle of Bull Run	**Battle of Antietam**
draft	**Emancipation Proclamation**
Battle of Gettysburg	

Union strategy for defeating the Confederacy during the Civil War

shutting off of an area by troops or ships to keep people and supplies from moving in or out

Civil War battle fought in 1862 near Sharpsburg, Maryland, that was an important victory for the Union

first major battle of the Civil War, fought near Manassas Junction, Virginia, on July 21, 1861

statement issued by President Abraham Lincoln on January 1, 1863, freeing all slaves in Confederate states still at war with the Union

law that requires men of a certain age to serve in the military, if called

Union victory over Confederate forces in 1863 in Gettysburg, Pennsylvania, that was a turning point in the Civil War

Gettysburg Address

Battle of Vicksburg

total war

assassination

Reconstruction

Thirteenth Amendment

black codes

Union victory over Confederate forces in 1863 at Vicksburg, Mississippi, that gave the Union control of the Mississippi River

Civil War speech given by President Abraham Lincoln in 1863 at the site of the Battle of Gettysburg

killing of a political or government leader

method of warfare that involves civilians as targets and is designed to destroy the opposing army and the people's will to fight

amendment to the United States Constitution that abolished slavery

period of rebuilding after the Civil War during which the Southern states rejoined the Union

laws that denied African Americans many civil rights

Freedmen's Bureau

Fourteenth Amendment

Fifteenth Amendment

impeachment

Jim Crow laws

segregation

sharecropping

amendment to the United States Constitution, ratified in 1868, that gave African Americans citizenship and equal protection under the law

federal agency set up in 1865 to provide food, schools, and medical care to freed slaves in the South

bringing of charges of wrongdoing against an elected official by the House of Representatives

amendment to the United States Constitution, ratified in 1870, that gave male citizens of all races the right to vote

separation of people of different races

laws passed in the South after Reconstruction enforcing the segregation of blacks and whites

system of farming in which farmers rent land and pay the landowner with a share of the crops they raise

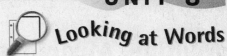
Build a Word

You can use prefixes and suffixes to build new words from a base word.

Prefix		Base Word		Suffix		Noun
trans-	+	continent	+	-al	→	transcontinental
"across"				"relating to"		"going across a continent"

Each of the words below is the base word for one of the vocabulary words from the unit. Using the prefixes and suffixes in the box, create a "formula" to help you build the vocabulary word. An example has been completed for you.

Prefixes:	in-	inter-	out-	re-	trans-	un-
Suffixes:	-al	-er	-ation	-ion	-ist	-ment

Base Word	Formula	Vocabulary Word
continent	trans- + continent + -al = transcontinental	transcontinental railroad
1. ride	_____	_____
2. reserve	_____	_____
3. settle	_____	_____
4. corporate	_____	_____

5. How many more words can you build? Use the prefixes and suffixes above to build other words. Write them on the lines below.

_____

_____

Notes for Home: Your child learned about how to build vocabulary words by using prefixes and suffixes.
Home Activity: Use a dictionary to look up the meanings of the prefixes and suffixes above. Then make a list of words that use those prefixes and suffixes.

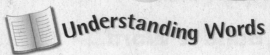

Multiple Meanings

Understanding Words

A single word may have more than one meaning. The word *express* may mean "to make something known" or "to represent by using a symbol." In **Pony Express**, *express* means "to send at a high speed." You can find all the meanings of a word by looking it up in a dictionary.

Different meanings are given for three vocabulary words below. For each sentence, write the number of the definition for the way the word is used in the sentence.

---

strike: 1. a refusal to work; **2.** to go; **3.** to attack by using force.

The soldiers were set to strike the enemy at midnight. _____

No mail was delivered during the postal strike. _____

I will strike off down the road to meet you. _____

---

reservation: 1. land set aside for Native Americans; **2.** a promise to keep something aside for someone's use; **3.** a misgiving or doubt or worry

Many Lakota crafts are sold on the reservation. _____

She had reservations about skydiving for the first time. _____

The couple had a reservation for dinner at eight. _____

---

telegraph: 1. a device for sending messages by wire; **2.** to send a telegram

The early telegraphs used Morse Code to send messages. _____

Will you telegraph me as soon as you arrive? _____

 Notes for Home: Today your child learned multiple meanings of vocabulary words from this unit.
Home Activity: Together with your child, make a list of words. Then look up the definitions for each word in a dictionary.

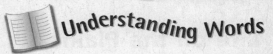

(Complete, Finish) Sentences

Understanding Words

Circle the term that best completes each sentence. Use the vocabulary cards if you need help.

1. In 1861, the Union Pacific and Central Pacific began construction of the (**Pony Express, transcontinental railroad**).

2. Cowboys used (**cattle drives, sodbusters**) to move longhorns across long distances.

3. A (**monopoly, corporation**) is a business owned by investors.

4. The (**Rough Riders, Buffalo Soldiers**) were African American fighters who fought in the wars against Native Americans on the Great Plains.

5. Pioneers willing to start farms on the Great Plains were able to get free land because of the (**Homestead Act, Battle of Little Big Horn**).

6. A (**corporation, monopoly**) has control of an entire industry and stops competition.

7. In (**settlement houses, labor unions**) workers joined together to improve wages and working conditions.

8. (**Exodusters, Homesteaders**) were settlers who claimed free land on the Great Plains.

9. The (**Pony Express, Rough Riders**) was a group of riders that delivered mail between Missouri and the West Coast.

10. Immigrants sometimes experienced the added hardship of (**tenements, prejudice**) when looking for work.

11. The Lakota Indians were forced to live on (**cattle drives, reservations**) by the United States government.

12. Jane Addams opened Hull House as a (**tenement, settlement house**) to help immigrants.

13. The town of Nicodemus, Kansas, was founded by African American pioneers who were also known as (**sodbusters, exodusters**).

14. The (**telegraph, barbed wire**) machine was used to send messages via electric wire.

 Notes for Home: Today your child selected the correct vocabulary word to complete vocabulary skills.
Home Activity: Have your child practice the vocabulary words in this activity by using them in sentences of his or her own.

Life on the Plains
Narrative Writing

The second half of the 1800s saw many settlers make their way west to the Great Plains. People came seeking cheap land and in the hopes of making a living through farming. Suppose it is 1880 and you and your family are newly arrived settlers on the Great Plains. Think about why you decided to start a new life in this unsettled land. Write a journal entry to describe the new land and the challenges you face. Use at least four words from the word box. You may use an additional sheet of paper.

Pony Express	**telegraph**	**transcontinental railroad**
Homestead Act	**homesteaders**	**sodbusters**
exodusters	**cattle drives**	**barbed wire**
reservation	**Battle of Little Big Horn**	

_____

_____

_____

_____

_____

_____

_____

_____

_____

_____

_____

Notes for Home: Today your child wrote a journal entry about the life of settlers on the Great Plains in the 1880s.
Home Activity: Together with your child, create a chart listing the pros and cons of moving to the Great Plains in the 1880s. Discuss reasons why people move today.

Pony Express	telegraph
transcontinental railroad	Homestead Act
homesteaders	sodbusters
exodusters	

machine used to send messages along wires using electricity

mail delivery service begun in 1860 that used a relay of riders on horses to carry mail from Missouri to California in ten days

law offering free land to pioneers willing to start farms on the Great Plains

Railroad that crosses an entire continent. The United States completed its first transcontinental railroad in 1869.

Great Plains farmers of the late 1800s who had to cut through the sod, or thick grass, before planting crops

settlers who claimed land in the Great Plains under the Homestead Act

name for African American pioneers who moved to the Great Plains after the Civil War

cattle drives	barbed wire
reservation	Battle of Little Bighorn
monopoly	corporation
tenement	

wire with sharp points used by farmers for fences

way cowboys moved huge herds of cattle from ranches in Texas to railroads in the late 1800s

Lakota victory over United States soldiers on June 25, 1876

land set aside by the United States government for Native Americans

business owned by investors

company that has control of an entire industry and stops competition

building that is divided into very small apartments

✂

prejudice	settlement house
labor union	strike
Spanish-American War	Rough Riders
Buffalo Soldiers	

center that provides help for immigrants or the poor

unfair negative opinion about a group of people

refusal of workers to work until business owners meet their demands

groups of workers joined together to gain improved working conditions and better wages

group of American volunteer soldiers during the Spanish-American War organized by Theodore Roosevelt

war in which the United States defeated Spain in 1898 and gained Spanish territory

nickname for African American soldiers who fought in the wars in the plains against Native Americans in the 1870s

Identify Nouns with Adjectives

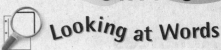
Looking at Words

The vocabulary words in the word box are each made up of two words. The first word is an adjective, because it describes the other word, which is a noun. Write each vocabulary word on the line next to the description of that adjective/noun combination. Then use your vocabulary cards to compare the actual definition of each vocabulary word.

Cold War	**New Deal**	**concentration camp**
United Nations	**World War II**	**Dust Bowl**
Great Migration	**Great Depression**	**Iron Curtain**
atomic bomb		

1. fresh bargain _____

2. large movement _____

3. joined countries _____

4. nuclear explosive _____

5. powdery hollow _____

6. chilly fight _____

7. crowded temporary shelters _____

8. high amount of inactivity _____

9. strong separator _____

10. global fight _____

 Notes for Home: Your child learned to recognize vocabulary words that are nouns with adjectives.
Home Activity: Challenge your child to make a list of two-word terms and to give a definition for each adjective/noun combination.

Alliances

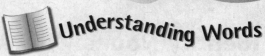
Understanding Words

Use a dictionary to find the definition of **alliance**. Many of this unit's vocabulary words name events, groups, and agreements that were the result of alliances among nations or groups of people. Complete each sentence below by writing the correct vocabulary word from the word box on the blank line. If you need more help, check your vocabulary cards and the discussion of each vocabulary word in the unit.

World War I	Nineteenth Amendment	Cuban Missile Crisis
Treaty of Versailles	League of Nations	Persian Gulf War
Progressives	Cold War	

1. President Wilson wanted to form an international **alliance** of countries called the _____.

2. An **alliance** of people called _____ fought for change in business practices and in government.

3. An **alliance** between the Soviet Union and Cuba led to the _____.

4. The **alliance** of women fighting for suffrage led to the passing of the _____.

5. The _____ was forced on Germany by the **alliance** of countries that won World War I.

6. The United States made **alliances** with democratic countries in its struggle with the Soviet Union during the _____.

7. The United States led an **alliance** of over 20 nations in the _____ against Iraq.

8. Two major **alliances** of countries directly led to the outbreak of _____ in 1914.

Notes for Home: Today your child associated vocabulary words with the vocabulary word **alliance**.
Home Activity: Discuss the importance of working together to help people achieve a goal. Look through a newspaper or news magazine with your child. Look for events that deal with present-day **alliances,** such as the United Nations, and discuss the goals they hope to achieve.

Name _____

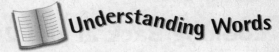

Missing Words

Write the missing words from the word box on the blanks in the sentences.

> dictator   isthmus   assembly line
>
> stock market   Harlem Renaissance   Progressives
>
> Holocaust   muckrakers   unemployment

1. On an _____, products are put together by many workers who add one piece at a time.

2. When factories produced more than they could sell, workers got laid off, leading to massive _____.

3. On the _____, people buy and sell shares in companies.

4. In the 1920s, African American culture bloomed in a period known as the _____.

5. To get from the Caribbean Sea to the Pacific Ocean, a canal was built across an _____ that connected North and South America.

6. President Roosevelt believed in the reform goals of the _____.

7. The Depression spread to Europe, where people in Germany and Italy were ready to hand over their freedoms to a _____ to solve their problems.

8. Reformers called _____ uncovered shameful business practices.

9. The destruction of the Jewish people became known as the _____, which means "widespread destruction."

Notes for Home: Today your child used context clues to identify the vocabulary words that belong in the sentences above.
Home Activity: Discuss with your child modern-day examples of the people, things, ideas, and events named by some of the vocabulary words in the above activity.

Looking Back at the 20th Century
Expository Writing

The United States was involved in a number of major events that affected the world in the second half of the twentieth century. Choose an event or period from the word box that you think is particularly interesting and important. Think about how the United States was involved, and what impact the event or period had on the world. Write to describe the event or period and explain its importance. You may use an additional sheet of paper.

arms control	arms race	atomic bomb	civil rights
Cold War	communism	Cuban Missile Crisis	Internet
Iron Curtain	Korean War	Persian Gulf War	space race
United Nations	Vietnam War	Watergate Scandal	

_____

_____

_____

_____

_____

_____

_____

_____

_____

_____

_____

_____

Notes for Home: Today your child wrote about an event or period from the second half of the twentieth century.
Home Activity: Ask your child to select another event from the list and explain its importance to you.

Progressives	muckraker
isthmus	World War I
alliance	League of Nations
Treaty of Versailles	Nineteenth Amendment
Great Migration	

writers and journalists who exposed shameful conditions in business and other areas of American life

reformers who wanted to improve government

War between the Allies and the Central Powers that lasted from 1914 to 1918. The United States joined the Allies in 1917, helping the Allies to win the war.

narrow strip of land that connects two larger areas

organization of nations formed after World War I

agreement between nations to defend one another

amendment to the Constitution giving women the right to vote, ratified in 1920

treaty signed in 1919 that officially ended World War I

movement between 1915 and 1940s of millions of African Americans to the North in search of work and fair treatment

© Scott Foresman 5

assembly line

Harlem Renaissance

unemployment

stock market

Great Depression

New Deal

Dust Bowl

dictator

World War II

cultural movement created in Harlem, an African American section of New York City

method of mass production in which the product is put together as it moves past a line of workers

organized market where stocks are bought and sold

number of workers who are without jobs

series of programs started by President Franklin D. Roosevelt to help the nation recover from the Great Depression

period of severe economic depression that began in 1929

leader with total power

period of severe drought in the 1930s that destroyed many farms on the Great Plains

War fought from 1939 to 1945 between the Allies and the Axis, and involving most of the countries in the world. The United States joined the Allies in 1941, helping the Allies gain victory.

concentration camp

Holocaust

atomic bomb

United Nations

communism

Cold War

Iron Curtain

Korean War

Cuban Missile Crisis

murder of six million Jews during World War II

prison in which the Nazis enslaved and murdered millions of people during World War II

international organization formed in 1945 to promote peace and end conflicts

powerful type of bomb with destructive forces of 20,000 tons of ordinary explosives

struggle between the United States and the Soviet Union that was fought with ideas, words, and money instead of soldiers

political and economic system in which the government owns all businesses and land

War between North Korea and South Korea lasting from 1950 to 1953. The United States fought with South Korea to stop the spread of communism.

imaginary border dividing Europe into communist and noncommunist countries after World War II

conflict between the United States and the Soviet Union over nuclear missiles in Cuba

arms race

civil rights

space race

Vietnam War

arms control

Watergate Scandal

Persian Gulf War

Internet

rights guaranteed to all citizens by the Constitution

countries hurrying to build more powerful weapons

war in the 1960s and 1970s in which the United States sent soldiers to South Vietnam to try to prevent communist forces from taking over the nation

race between the United States and the Soviet Union to explore outer space during the Cold War

scandal that forced President Richard Nixon to resign from office in 1974

agreement to limit the production of weapons

worldwide network of computers; became popular in the 1990s

war involving the United States and its allies against Iraq in 1991